MW01717085

HOPE IS A PERSON

Hope Is a Person: An Advent Devotional

Published 2022 by Acoma Press

Requests for information should be addressed to:

Acoma Press
40 W. Littleton Blvd. Suite 210, PMB 215
Littleton, CO 80120

www.acomapress.org
info@acomapress.org

Cover Design & Interior Layout: Evan Skelton

Cover Illustration: iStock.com/SweetGrace

First Printing, 2022

Printed in the United States of America

Paperback ISBN: 979-8-9872145-0-3
PDF ISBN: 979-8-9872145-1-0

DEDICATION

2022 marks the first Christmas without my dad. He passed away in May 2022. Like many people, I have celebrated every Christmas of my life with my parents in some way on some level.

Those times of opening Christmas presents with my parents never disappointed. Somehow, they always knew what my brother and I wanted. And, somehow, there was always this one, big, main gift that would leave us speechless.

In 2022, with the loss of my dad, I celebrate Christmas because of the hope that I have in Jesus that I will see dad again. I celebrate Christmas, because while this is my first Christmas without my dad, it is his first Christmas in the presence of Jesus. I celebrate Christmas because I know without a doubt that my dad is celebrating Christmas like he never has before.

CONTENTS

ACKNOWLEDGEMENTS

I am grateful for all of those who have made this devotional possible!

First and foremost, my wife Jenna who is my partner in life, parenting, ministry and every other endeavor. I would not be who I am without her.

My daughters Madison, Emma, Avery and Charlotte. My son in-law Braden and my two grandsons, Luke and Ezra. Each of you are a reminder of God's many good gifts to me!

My Dad and Mom, Larry and Cherrie Edwards. Both of my parents encouraged me to write at an early age. No doubt they have both contributed to my love of writing.

Kelly Hall. Thank you for your insights and edits. I am grateful.

Garrett Wishall. Thank you for your perspective and contributions to this project. You have made this devotional so much better.

INTRODUCTION

Our plans for our Christmas celebration in 2008 were all set. We would celebrate the Christmas Eve service at our church, open presents with our kids on Christmas morning, and then make the short drive to Bethlehem, Pennsylvania for the rest of Christmas day.

Once in Bethlehem, we had a full slate of things we planned to do. We would experience so many of the things that are associated with Christmas. Everything in the entire town would be decorated for Christmas. Christmas lights would adorn all the streets and stores. There would be shops where the kids could decorate gingerbread cookies and horse carriages to ride across this historic town that comes to life at Christmas. It had all the potential to be an ideal, picture-perfect Christmas.

But we never made it to Bethlehem.

My wife Jenna had an appointment with her doctor on December 23. She was 27 weeks pregnant with our third daughter and her pregnancy had been smooth up until this point. At the appointment, however, the doctor expressed some concern about Jenna's feet being swollen.

We were initially not that worried. Yet, a few hours later, we were at the hospital where they were monitoring

Jenna's blood pressure. One thing led to another, and we ended up spending the night at the hospital. I still remember Jenna and I discussing whether or not we should cancel the hotel reservations for our Pennsylvania trip. Not too much later, we learned that Jenna had preeclampsia and that her blood pressure was rising. Even after the doctors told us about what was going on with Jenna's body, we did not quite understand the impact that this diagnosis would have. I remember thinking out loud together that she may have to stay in bed for the remainder of the pregnancy. In the back of our minds, though, we still thought we would be going home in time for Christmas.

Little by little, we began to realize just how serious things were.

We cancelled the Christmas Eve service. We cancelled the trip to Bethlehem. We spent Christmas Eve in the hospital, and our two older daughters stayed with some friends.

The next morning, we called the girls and listened over the phone as they opened their Christmas presents. Later Christmas morning, the doctor came in and told us that they would have to deliver the baby soon.

Mere hours later, Avery Hope Edwards was born.

Avery weighed 2 pounds and 4 ounces. To put it in perspective of how small Avery was on her birthday, I was able to put her hand through my wedding ring and move it all the way up to her elbow.

Avery was moved to the neonatal intensive care unit on the first floor. Jenna was moved to the intensive care unit on the seventh floor.

In retrospect, I wish that I could say that I handled all of this well. It would feel good if I could say that I took everything in stride. But that is not what took place.

My wife was in intensive care and was not doing well. My daughter was in the NICU and hooked up to several machines. Our other two daughters were at home worried and scared.

From moment to moment, I did not know where I was supposed to be. When I was with Jenna, she would want to know how Avery was doing. When I was with Avery, I would worry about how Jenna was doing. I wore out the hospital elevator those first couple of days. I could not ever be settled in one spot. I was even more unsettled on the inside.

Do not get me wrong, I knew God was there. While I was uncertain about everything, I did believe that God cared about the circumstances. I knew there were thousands of people praying for us and for the entire situation. I was thankful for the hundreds of emails from people assuring us of their prayers and concerns. Yet, in the moment, all I saw and felt was chaos and confusion.

I was a Christian. I was the Pastor. I knew the answers. I thought I knew what to tell others who were in the middle of a crisis. But, on the inside, I was falling apart.

I was sad. I was confused. I was angry. I was helpless.

A few days after Christmas, I walked out of the hospital elevator and leaned against a wall. I had come to the realization that I knew that I had no power. I was painfully aware that I had no control whatsoever.

As much as I tried, as much as I worried, as much as I asserted whatever will I had in me, I realized that I was completely powerless to make anything happen. I recognized that I had no capacity to fix anything at all.

But, leaning up against that wall at Winthrop Hospital in Mineola, New York, I remember feeling the Lord comforting me. I remember His gentle whisper to my soul. I remember the Lord assuring me that He loved Jenna, that He loved Avery, and that He loved me. I remember walking away from that wall believing that God's love for us was more than I could possibly understand.

Christmas of 2008 is when I began to have a better understanding of what we really celebrate at Christmas. The love that God has for us is in Christ is deeper and stronger than we can imagine.

We celebrate that Jesus came into our world of chaos and confusion giving the comfort and order that comes with His presence.

We celebrate that Jesus came to earth in the midst of our powerlessness with infinite strength and ability.

We celebrate that Jesus came to share His love, show His love and spread His love to every person on our planet.

Christmas of 2008 is when I began to have a greater grasp on what hope really is. Hope is not wishful thinking or simply positive thoughts. Hope is a confident expectation that God will always act according to His character and will always fulfill His promises. Hope enables a growing faith that I can relinquish control and let God do God's job. Hope expresses itself in a deep trust that God is greater than my problems and my inability to manage them.

Jesus has shown us that hope can exist in the midst of any circumstance because God is with us. Hope is a person because Jesus is the Way, the Truth and the Life. Hope is a person because Jesus knows the road we walk and has walked it Himself. Hope is a person because Jesus invites into the meaningful, personal relationship with God we all need.

It's out of this experience that I have written this devotional. This experience has changed and shaped the way I understand Christmas. The purpose of this devotional is to lead us to come face to face with the reality of why we so desperately need a Savior. The purpose of this devotional is to lead us to avoid glossing over our difficulties and sugar-coating certain aspects of the Christmas.

It is my prayer that this devotional will lead you to celebrate the significance of this Christmas Season. It is my prayer that you would embrace the full meaning of what it is that we are actually celebrating this Christmas. It is my prayer that your hope would be renewed, your faith would be encouraged, and that you would worship our Savior and King, Jesus Christ.

DECEMBER 1

In this the love of God was made manifest among us, that God sent his only Son into the world, so that we might live through him. – **1 John 4:9**

A few years ago, a news story came out of Santa Clarita, California, about a woman who returned her non-artificial Christmas tree to Costco. The explanation that she provided for returning the Christmas tree on January 4, was that the Christmas tree was dead. Her assessment was not inaccurate, the Christmas tree was in fact dead and had been since the day she bought it. To add to the absurdity, Costco awarded the woman a full refund! It is a crazy story.

Metaphorically speaking, this story speaks to the not-so-glamorous parts of our spiritual journey. How many times have we looked for life, purpose or pleasure from something that was dead? We do it more often than we realize.

We turn to things looking for life outside of our relationship with God, thinking that whatever or whoever it is will make us feel better, or if not, perhaps at least numb us out to our pain and suffering.

We use all kinds of things to temporarily, immediately, impulsively and/or compulsively escape our current reality. It is not just the well-known addictions that earn us a seat in anonymous rooms like alcohol and drug abuse, eating disorders or sex and love addictions. It is any person, place, situation or thing we allow to determine whether we have peace and joy.

Maybe our dead Christmas tree is a certain amount of money, a particular job title or a relationship that we believe will give us what we need. We might even trick ourselves by dressing it up with fancy lights and shimmering ornaments to give us the illusion that it is alive. Time and again, however, we end up undressing the tree and hauling a once fresh and fragrant tree out to the trash pile. These types of illusions do not last, and the feeling they may offer at the beginning is not sustainable.

No matter how many times we ask for something spiritually dead to give us life, meaning and purpose, the outcome will always be the same.

So, what do we do in response to this repeated and continual outcome?

We can take a cue from the lady at Costco and bring __________ to God.

We can share our experience with God, we can say we tried __________ in order to gain __________ and it ultimately failed to produce what we imagined.

That will not be a surprise to God. He is not going to ask for proof of purchase, He already knows. God knew it so well that He instructed us, warned us and reminded us of what gives life and what does not.

While confession and repentance are very uncomfortable, utterly humiliating and vulnerable, it is also a place where the Lord can go to work.

With our dead tree out of the way, we can welcome more light into our places of darkness, and we can stop trying to dress up our failures. As we confess, God pours out more of His abundant grace.

The season of Christmas celebrates this penetration of darkness by the Light of God. The birth and presence of Jesus gives us tangible comfort and restores hope that joy is once again possible.

- How can you embrace the grace Jesus is extending to you as you enter this Christmas season?

- When you pause to meet God in this moment, where do you sense His Light entering in?

DECEMBER 2

I pray that God, the source of all hope, will infuse your lives with an abundance of joy and peace in the midst of your faith so that your hope will overflow through the power of the Holy Spirit. **– Romans 15:13**

Every single day we get more than our fair share of bad news. Sometimes things do not ease up. There is no shortage of misery to be found; at times the headlines seem almost too shocking to comprehend — our minds cannot fully process the weight of all of it.

We may not think that the chaos taking place around us can get any worse — and that is without adding to it our own personal issues and problems. Our marriages, children, parents, jobs and finances are just a few of the things that keep us awake at night, fill us with anxiety and contribute to our own personal chaos. The issues that we are facing and dealing with on various levels make it easy to become numb to breaking news that seems to constantly blow up our phones with notifications.

Having access to crisis on a global scale can make us cynical and jaded, sometimes afraid to live. Too much bad news hardens our hearts, weakens our hope and dampens our spirits. But, as hard as the world seems, waking up to bad news is nothing new.

- People did not recently become chaotic.
- People did not wake up harsher than ever.
- People did not suddenly hurl themselves head long into evil.

Where there are people, there is the stuff that people get into, go through and lash out with.

As we celebrate this Christmas season, we cannot shut out the truth that there are difficult and devastating things taking place all around us and within us. But we must learn to hold the darkness with the light, we must open ourselves while enduring the urge to contract in misery. Rework this sentence, what do you mean by hold the darkness with the light?

Jesus entered into this dark world thousands of years ago.

- He came to be with us in the thick of our chaos.
- He came to be with us in our darkest hour.
- He came to be with us in the midst of our sorrows.
- He came to be with us.

When Jesus entered, hope entered. Sometimes we lose hope because we focus more on the problem than the solution. When our lives feel out of control internally or externally, we must learn to look for God at work in our midst. When we can do that, we will find the hope and peace we are looking for.

- Where are you experiencing chaos in your life right now?

- When you pause to meet God in the moment, where do you sense God at work?

DECEMBER 3

Therefore, preparing your minds for action, and being sober-minded, set your hope fully on the grace that will be brought to you at the revelation of Jesus Christ.

– 1 Peter 1:13

Anticipation is a big part of the Christmas season! Do you remember a Christmas when you were expecting a particular present? Maybe it was a present that you had requested directly or something you strongly hinted or dropped obvious clues about.

As you unwrap the presents, your mind is only on one thing. You take off bows, tear open the red and green paper and wonder if This. Is. It. Is this the present you were waiting for?

Time after time it is not. You have felt the anticipation grow as you opened present after present that was not it, and then it is over. You look at all of the gifts people gave you, and you are thankful for them, but you missed out on really receiving them because you were fixated on how great you were going to feel getting "the one." You may even try to go back to them, unbox them and get the initial thrill back, but you still have the negative charge associated with that feeling of something missing because your focus was on getting a certain thing and not the intended love behind the things you got.

As much as we can place our hope and anticipation on something and someone, there are a lot of us who have placed our hopelessness and apprehension on something or someone as well. As things or people fail to meet our expectations, we become disappointed, jaded and cynical about anything that promises hope but disappoints, and we carry all of this hopelessness into all that we do and everywhere we go.

So how do we stay focused on the anticipation of Christ and not things? How do we not miss love? How do we not lose hope?

- We receive Jesus in the moment.
- We invite Jesus into our skepticism.
- We surrender to Jesus our failed expectations.
- We lean into the Light of Christ and ask God to help us see that even when we abandon hope, hope does not abandon us.

God never loses hope in us.

- No matter what we have done.
- No matter where we have been.
- No matter how far away from Him we feel.
- No matter what anyone else thinks.
- No matter what anyone else says.

- No matter how many chances we have blown.
- No matter how many times you have disappointed you.

Whether or not it is tangible for you today, there is more than enough hope in the world because Jesus entered in.

- What is your hope for this Christmas Season?

- Spend some time journaling your intentions for the season.

DECEMBER 4

We love because he first loved us. **- 1 John 4:19**

While we enjoy and celebrate the Christmas season, we also know that there is pressure that comes with it. Maybe we want our house, yard or Christmas tree to be decorated in a particular way. Maybe it is the numerous parties, recitals and concerts that make for an especially busy Christmas season. Or maybe we are worried about finding the perfect gifts for everyone.

Maybe no pressure compares to when we are caught not having a gift for someone else.

It may go something like this: someone you never would have expected surprises you with a Christmas gift. They hand you a present that is perfectly gift-wrapped and tied with shimmering ribbons with your name on the gift tag. You give them an appreciative look, trying your hardest to hide your panic, but you are starting to perspire, and although you are genuinely thankful for their generosity, inside you are freaking out because you know that you have nothing to give them in return.

There is something about receiving a gift that leaves us desperately wanting to reciprocate. It only seems right and fair. Someone gives us something and we give them something back. This works best when the gifts have a similar value. When someone gives us something that is worth about $20, we do not want to give them something so small that we are seen as cheap or so big that we make them feel uncomfortable.

Reciprocation makes sense to a lot of us.

And yet, the joy of Christmas is that we have been given an incredible gift in Jesus that is hard to comprehend much less measure, because it never stops giving.

God has given us a gift beyond anything we could repay. Jesus' arrival is the incarnation of God breaking through to us with incredible peace, indescribable grace and an incomparable love that goes beyond anything that we can earn or achieve on our own.

Christmas is not only the season of giving; it is the season of receiving also. If receiving an unexpected gift from a stranger without having one to give in return creates unease, it is certainly not unimaginable that we would struggle to fully open up to what God has for us when we have no idea how to reciprocate in response to the gift of His Son. What do you give someone who has everything?

We make our giving more complicated than it is.

We have a God who gives us love, presence, comfort, peace, joy, hope, and forgiveness in full measure. We cannot repay Him. Instead, God calls us to receive our identity as His beloved son or daughter and respond with heartfelt worship. Such worship is on display when the fruit of the Spirit characterizes our attitude and actions: love, joy, peace, patience, goodness, faithfulness, gentleness and self-control.

Simple, but not easy.

We love God because He first loved us. We serve God not to repay Him, but because Jesus first served us. We worship God by allowing him to grow our faith and take the news of His love to others.

In all of these ways, we have the chance and opportunity to give to the Giver.

- What way(s) do you respond to God that gives you the most life?

- What ways are the most challenging?

DECEMBER 5

Again Jesus spoke to them, saying, "I am the light of the world. Whoever follows me will not walk in darkness, but will have the light of life." **– 1 John 4:19**

As people we like to be right, but there are times when that desire rises to the level of need. Several years ago, I saw this play out in front of our apartment in Brooklyn. At about 6:30 in the morning, I heard a commotion coming from outside. Looking out the window I noticed a man complaining to anyone and everyone who would listen. After a few moments, it was clear that he had received a parking ticket for parking too close to the fire hydrant. It was also clear that he strongly objected to the citation.

I watched the man make his case to a couple of different people. He repeatedly explained how the ticket was undeserved and unjust. After what seemed like a long time, I pulled away from the window ready to move on with the day, thinking this had run its course.

I was wrong. Hours later, the irate citizen was still verbally pleading his case to no particular person. He went so far as to retrieve a measuring tape to measure the distance from the front of his car to the fire hydrant. He even took pictures from various angles all in an effort to prove he did not deserve the ticket. He believed what he saw was right regardless of the piece of paper on his windshield telling him otherwise.

Some of us know exactly what this is like. We know we want to be right. We want to convince others are we are right. We fight to justify ourselves. We argue to make our case. We want to portray to ourselves and to others that we are absolutely right.

Yet, Scripture tells us tells us that apart from God, our own attempts at righteousness will not set us free. We need God's Light to see what our shortcomings are. We need God's help to show us our utter helplessness apart from Him, to show us how wrong we really are.

Jesus brought in God's Light as the Light of the Word. Jesus teaches us how to see what is really going on. Jesus shows us, and is, the Way, the Truth and the Life.

- As you ponder Christmas and all that it means, spend some time asking Jesus for more light to see things as He sees them.

- Reflect on how the righteousness of Jesus is not dependent upon our own righteousness.

DECEMBER 6

For to us a child is born,
to us a son is given;
and the government shall be upon his shoulder,
and his name shall be called
Wonderful Counselor, Mighty God,
Everlasting Father, Prince of Peace.

- Isaiah 9:6

One of the fun elements of the Christmas season is surprising someone with a particular present you know they really want. Maybe it is something you recalled your spouse mentioning during a passing conversation in September. Maybe it is a gift that your child would have never asked for he or she thought it was way too expensive. Or maybe it was in a letter your child had written to Santa Claus.

When we pull off such a surprise, we feel like we are on top of the world!

No matter how well you hide it, disguise it or dress it up, God is not surprised by who we are or what we do. God is never thrown off by our shortcomings, failures, dashed plans, addictions and lack of satisfaction and peace. God fully understands why we do what we do because He knows us.

God knows why we sometimes feel empty, act out, withdraw, complain, spread negativity and bottom out and He loves us in the midst of our brokenness and through to the other side.

What I hear in Isaiah's message is that we can trust God to be who he says he is: the one who knows us fully and completely and will meet our every need through Christ.

- Before we knew that we needed compassion, God sent us a Wonderful Counselor.
- Before we knew we needed to be held and feel secure, He sent a Mighty God.
- Before we knew we would need help growing up, God sent an Everlasting Father.
- Before we knew life was full of battles, God sent the Prince of Peace.

We can entrust God with who we are and come to Him honestly and openly. In Christ, He knows us, and He loves us.

Now it is our turn to stand in awe.

- What is one thing you are trying to hide or hold back from God?

- How can you grow in trusting God fully today?

DECEMBER 7

And the angel said to them, "Fear not, for behold, I bring you good news of great joy that will be for all the people."

- Luke 2:10

Adam and Eve heard the voice,
They were convinced,
They made the choice,
They thought made sense.

It turned out
they had bought a lie,
As God came about
they tried to hide.

There was blame,
There was a curse,
There was shame,
But something worse.

The cycle of sin
Would contaminate us all,
The world was broken,
This was the Fall.

Sin had entered
and taken its hold,
Like the darkness of winter
and the bitterness of cold.

Still, it was not the end,
God had a plan.
Death He would rend,
Through the Life of One Man.

While there is pain to mourn,
And while we have tried to cope,
We celebrate that a baby was born,
Who became our Hope.

Adam and Eve saw that tree,
The Deceiver presented them with a choice,
Similarly, you and me
Are familiar with that voice.

Out of our sin,
A child born was born to be our Savior,
A child who would become the man,
Who changed everything forever,

That's why the angels sang loud
the night God sent His Son,
"Tell all the crowds,
Joy to the world! The Lord is come!"

DECEMBER 8

But seek first the kingdom of God and his righteousness, and all these things will be added to you. – **Matthew 6:33**

What do you want for Christmas?

Many of us are familiar with this question. We have been asked this question most of our lives.

We have heard it from our parents when we were kids. We have heard it while sitting on Santa's lap at the shopping mall. Some of us have been asked to write letters to the North Pole to answer this question.

In later years, as parents, we ask the same question to our kids. We care about they want. When possible, we look forward to giving them the gift they truly want to receive.

But, over the years, the question has become more difficult for me to answer.

It is not that I am against receiving anything. It is not that I am against having any type of possessions. It is just that the actual gift is less important to me than the intentions of the one who is giving me the gift.

If one of my daughters ask me what I want for Christmas, I can say without hesitation that I want whatever you want me to have. The giver of the gift has become more important to me than the gift itself.

I want the same to be true in my relationship with Jesus. I want to have the same attitude. I want to know and trust that He knows what I want and need better than I do. Even more than that, He knows that I have wanted things that were not good and maybe not what I thought I wanted.

We can go after things we do not need.

We can pursue things that would not be good for us.

And when we actually get them, we realize we want nothing to do with them.

The arrival of Jesus leads us to understand that Jesus knows what we want and need far better than we do. What I want to want for Christmas this year and every year is His way, His plan and His direction. Instead of endlessly searching for satisfaction in a gift, I want to look to trust in the Giver of all good gifts.

The choice awaits us each day. Today, may we want to want Jesus more.

- What keeps you from wanting what Jesus wants for you?

- Ask God to change your wants to His wants.

DECEMBER 9

The Lord will rescue me from every evil deed and bring me safely into his heavenly kingdom. To him be the glory forever and ever. Amen. **- 2 Timothy 4:18**

Christmas is a big deal to every kid. But, as I noted in my introduction, our daughter Avery also has a birthday on December 25. That means she is always a little extra excited about all of the details and discussions that go with how we are celebrating that special day.

Typically, the Christmas presents for our daughters are wrapped in four different types of wrapping paper to help keep track of who the presents are for without the girls knowing. As our girls have gotten older, they have been known to collaborate in trying to determine who the gifts are for. Avery closely examines all of the presents, and without touching the gifts, she is intent on determining which of them are for her.

There is one present that Avery keeps looking at intently. She walks up to the tree and stares at this one particular present. She just knows that it is for her. She is positive. She imagines what it could be. She asks all kinds of questions. She pleads for just one hint.

Jenna and I smile at her. We are very content to keep her in wonder.

Honestly, we were having some fun at her expense. We were leading her to believe that there was something wrapped in the box that she wanted. We were even insinuating that the gift was indeed hers.

Still, we know the truth. That present is not for her. That gift that she is so certain is hers is absolutely not.

We have intentionally deceived our precious, sweet, and amazing daughter.

The wrapping paper is nothing but a decoy.

We know what she does not know.

We even know that she really does not even want the gift inside the gift-wrapped box that she thinks she wants.

This is part of the reason why Christmas is so important.

- We think we know what we are doing.
- We think we know what we want.
- We think we have outsmarted everyone else.
- We think we have things figured out.
- We think we have it all together.

We end up calling the shots and doing things our own way.

Yet inevitably we find that we do not know what we think we know.

What we thought we wanted was not what it was cracked up to be.

We go after what we thought would bring us happiness and fulfillment, only to be disappointed when we discover what it really is.

The celebration of Christmas is that Jesus came to rescue us from us.

Jesus came to rescue us from our disappointment, our deception, and our doubt.

Jesus has come to heal us from the hurt and pain that we have endured, as we sought to have our lives fulfilled by things that could never fulfill us.

But there is one other thing about Christmas:

- Jesus is the gift that does satisfy.
- Jesus never disappoints.
- Jesus never under-delivers.
- Jesus never overpromises.
- Jesus Himself is the gift.

All of us have been deceived to the point that we placed our hope in something or someone that could not deliver what it had promised.

But, remarkably, in sheer mercy and grace,

Jesus delivers hope that will never diminish and will never disappoint.

- What are ways that you have seen others deceived?

- What are ways that you have been deceived?

- What are ways that hope in Jesus has rescued you from being deceived?

DECEMBER 10

And the angel said to them, "Fear not, for behold, I bring you good news of great joy that will be for all the people."

- Luke 2:10

One Christmas morning I was out buying batteries at our local gas station. I am confident that I paid about four times more for these batteries than I would have paid at Wal-Mart, but we had an immediate situation where to enjoy a new favorite toy we needed batteries to make it come to life. Twenty minutes later, the problem was solved.

Simple fixes that elevate you to hero status are a fun part of being a dad. But, after nearly 30 years of marriage and as the father of four daughters, I have learned the hard way that there is a limit to my dad-superpowers. I cannot solve all of the issues and problems that arise in life.

When I see one of my girls worrying, I want to tell them why they do not have to worry.

When I see one of my girls upset, I want to tell them why they do not have to be upset.

When I see one of my girls struggling with anything, I want to tell them it does not have to be so complicated. I want to fix it. I want to make it better. I want to make the problem go away. I want to make them better. I want to fix them.

One of the most sobering realities to discover as a parent is that there are some situations that we cannot fix. A second more sobering reality is that when our children experience uneasiness, so do we.

Maybe fixing them will fix me. Maybe fixing their issues will get me back to feeling peace and joy.

Is it even about them? It is often we who are the most uncomfortable in other's pain. I cannot sit in other's problems without wanting to relieve myself by relieving them.

I want to fix things. I want to make things better. I want problems to go away.

It is even more difficult when hard things happen during a season we set aside for hope, joy and celebration. But struggles do not take holidays. During the holiday season, we see people hurting, mourning, longing and living without hope. We experience people dealing with loss, death and what might have been. And as much as we want to fix their problems, we are powerless to do so.

Understanding our powerlessness to fix people frees us to point them to the One who can.

The One who sees. The One who knows. The One who heals. The One who comforts. The One who entered our brokenness, not just to fix us, but to make us new.

What people need is for us to conduct the light and comfort of Christ. They need a place and people they can be real with, who allow them to be just who they are and their situation to be just what it is. We can be present in people's pain. We can share our hope in Christ. We can pray for them to believe.

There are some situations and circumstances that only God can fix.

- What is a circumstance in your life you know of that only God can resolve?

- What is a situation that you are trying to control that you need to relinquish to God?

DECEMBER 11

"Glory to God in the highest, and on earth peace among those with whom he is pleased!" - **Luke 2:14**

In December 2006, we were celebrating our first Christmas in New York. As we were exploring and becoming more familiar with New York City, we discovered that ABC's "Good Morning America" television show was looking for kids to take part in their Christmas morning programming. We decided to sign up our daughters Madison and Emma and all of us went down a week before Christmas for the pre-recording of the show and to spend the entire day in Manhattan.

We showed up at the ABC studios in Times Square to an incredible display of Christmas decorations. Christmas lights were glowing all around the set and poinsettias lined the span of the stage. Diane Sawyer and Robin Roberts were decked out in Christmas attire and Patti Labelle sang an incredibly beautiful Christmas song. Then there were our stars of the show, Madison and Emma, who were dressed in their Christmas best sitting quietly on the floor in the middle of about 20 or so other children who were watching the show.

As you can imagine, to the mind it was like Christmas. Everything that was happening was implying that it actually was Christmas. It almost felt like Christmas morning. But that was not the case.

In America, we have dressed up Christmas to the max. On one hand, it feels honoring to its importance. On the other hand, it seems to make the sacred profane.

I am not knocking Christmas decorations, music, trees or any of the other fun elements that go along with Christmas. But I have also had times when my experience of all the glitz and glamor was more like the "Good Morning America" version of Christmas instead of an authentic celebration of our Savior's birth.

Christmas is an anointed, sacred time. Again, we are not wrong for celebrating with presents, parties and extensive preparation, as long as it adds to or brings awareness of the significance of Jesus' birth instead of distracting and detracting from it.

At Christmas there is light, community, honor and homage, giving and receiving and most important of all the remembering of the most important element of all: Jesus, Immanuel, God with us on earth.

His coming brings light and life and a hope that will never disappoint.

My thought in is how do we remain present to sacredness of the season in the hustle and bustle of it all?

- What are some ways that we can keep from "going through the motions" this Christmas season?

- What is a way to intentionally celebrate this Christmas season with authenticity?

DECEMBER 12

the people dwelling in darkness
have seen a great light,
and for those dwelling in the region and shadow of death,
on them a light has dawned."

- Matthew 4:16

The lighting of the Rockefeller Christmas Tree has become a symbol for welcoming in the Christmas Season in New York City. This yearly ritual has officially been taking place since 1933, with nearly 125 million people visiting the Rockefeller Tree each year.

Several years ago, the Rockefeller tree again came to life in all of its glory. Millions of people watched the ceremony on television as celebrities performed songs to welcome in the Christmas season. During that same time, however, there was another news headline that broke at Rockefeller Center that revealed brokenness amid the celebration.

Within the shadow of the glowing Christmas Tree festivities at Rockefeller Plaza, NBC Studios was working in high gear to address the fallout from several sexual harassment allegations against one of its' broadcasters. In the middle of the Christmas season, the darkness of sin and its' consequences was on display.

Of course, this particular celebrity was not alone. At that point, several other high-profile men had been fired for exploiting their power and position over women in the workplace. Without a doubt, there have been hundreds of others in the months and years that have followed. We can only imagine the hundreds of lives that have been flipped upside down as a result of these actions. Life for many will never go back to what it was before.

These high-profile cases only go to show that no one has it all together. We all have dark sides. Many of us have encountered similar situations where our lives seemingly became tragically chaotic because of sinful choices we have made. Some of us know the very real struggle of dealing with our own self-inflicted damage to our relationships and our own lives.

It is out of the dreadfulness of this darkness and the hopelessness of these situations that we are reminded once again of why Christmas is so important. Not the Gwen Stefani rocking around the Christmas Tree at Rockefeller Center kind of Christmas. Not the Santa Claus at Macy's kind of Christmas. The real Christmas.

The Christmas where God stepped into our world and supplied provision for our every need from the trivial to the seemingly insurmountable.

Christmas is about God providing us with a Savior. Christmas is about the celebration of the grace we have been given. Christmas is about the reconciliation with God that is now available to us because of what Jesus has done for us.

Christmas does not call us to put aside the messiness of our lives. Christmas is not about cleaning ourselves up, putting on a mask and a smile and hiding all of the wrong things we have done. Christmas is the celebration that a Redeemer has come to rescue us in the middle of our hurt, sin and shame.

If you are ever in New York City, you should definitely go by the Rockefeller Center and see the beautifully adorned Christmas Tree with all of its lights. It is without a doubt a beautiful sight to behold. And, as you are looking upward, may you be reminded that "the people dwelling in darkness have seen a great light" (Matt. 4:16b).

- Do you recall a Christmas when you were trying just to get through it?

- How can you rest in the provision of Jesus this Christmas season?

- What is one way that God has provided for you this Christmas season?

DECEMBER 13

The light shines in the darkness, and the darkness has not overcome it. **- John 1:5**

Maybe you have been around a kid who wanted a particular present for Christmas. They have been asking for the present for months. They drop some not so subtle hints about where the gift can be found, how much it costs and why it is such a great value.

Those of who have been a parent in these situations and scenarios go to great lengths to keep our kids guessing. Maybe we pretend that we are not going to be able to get them the present. Maybe we try to temper their expectations. Maybe we even take measures to wrap the gift in a box that makes them think for a moment that they are getting a new griddle or some other household appliance!

It can be a lot of fun to lead or mislead our kids when it comes to expectations revolving around Christmas gifts, but in many other parts of our lives, we respond differently to deception. We do not find it amusing to be intentionally deceived. We do not see the humor in being fooled. We definitely do not like the misrepresentation of the way things actually are.

It makes sense that so many of us are cynical. We question the authenticity of something or somebody. It is understandable why so many of us are skeptical. We know what it is like to have something or someone not deliver what it claims to deliver.

We do not want to be fooled. We do not want to be taken. We do not want to be burned. We do not want to be gullible.

It is hard for us to take something at face value. It is hard to believe. It is easy to question. It is easy to have doubts.

After a while, anything good seems too good to be true, yet the precise thing that God asks of us is to trust Him.

- Trust Him without knowing the outcome.
- Trust Him in spite of the odds.
- Trust Him that He can do what He says He will do.
- Trust Him that He is able.

God does not always do things on our terms, in our time frame or in the way we think He should.

Still, God has never broken a promise. God has never underperformed. God has never been late. God has never been caught off guard.

It is easier to be cynical than to trust, and yet that is the invitation that God extends to us today.

Trust. Trust him. Trust him today. Trust him today with everything.

- What is one thing you have been hesitant to trust God with?

- How can you begin trusting God with that one thing today?

DECEMBER 14

And the Word became flesh and dwelt among us, and we have seen his glory, glory as of the only Son from the Father, full of grace and truth. - **John 1:14**

YOU CAME

You heard us crying,
And you came.
You saw us trying,
And you came.

You knew we were dying,
And you came.
Even when we were lying,
You came.

When we were hiding,
You came.
When we were denying,
You came.

You came to set us free,
You came to make us whole,
You came to our rescue,
You came for our souls.

You came to be human,
And show up in our shame.
You came to enlighten,
And relieve us of blame.

You so loved the world,
That is why you came.
Your name is Jesus,
The Name above all Names!

Because you came,
We can confide,
Because you came,
We can abide,

Because you came,
We no longer have to hide,
Because you came,
we have you to walk alongside.

DECEMBER 15

The next day he saw Jesus coming toward him, and said, "Behold, the Lamb of God, who takes away the sin of the world! **- John 1:29**

Many years ago, we brought our daughters to see Santa Claus at the Macy's in Manhattan. If ever I was going to have high expectations for a visit with Santa Claus, this was it! Maybe it was from watching "Miracle on 34th Street." Maybe it was because this was New York City. Maybe it was because the line was nearly three hours long to see Santa. In any case, I strongly suspected that this would be the most legitimate experience of Santa I would ever have.

We waited and waited in the line. My wife Jenna and I encouraged our girls that it was going to be worth the wait, all the while looking at one another and simultaneously "this had better be worth the wait."

As we inched closer to the finish line of seeing the "as close as it gets to a real Santa" there is we eventually came to a change to the line that I had not expected. (You can stop reading now if you would rather remain disillusioned about seeing Santa Claus at Macy's in Manhattan.)

The line to see Santa Claus unexpectedly broke off into five or six other lines. I was confused. I said to Jenna, "Why do they break off the single line into five or six lines, it is not going to make the process of seeing Santa go by any faster. We are still going to have to wait just as long!"

Jenna looked at me somewhat disappointed and worried that I had not quite figured out that there was not just one Macy's Santa Claus, but at least five or six at any given time.

This experience echoes in my mind as I think about my life spiritually. If I am not careful and deliberate about trusting and following Jesus as my only priority, I can have five or six other priorities in my life contending for equal time, attention and importance at any given moment.

When knowing and following Jesus is not my singular focus, I make a lot of other things my focus. When worshipping and abiding in Jesus is not my top priority, I make a lot of other things my top priority. When I live my life like Jesus is not enough for me, I look to a lot of other things in an attempt to fill the void and I begin looking to anything and everything to provide me with what I think will be enough, what I think will make me happy and what I think will provide me with satisfaction.

But nothing and no one other than Jesus can.

Jesus is the One who sits enthroned next to God the Father and who is worthy of praise. Jesus is the only person who brings life, salvation, forgiveness and redemption. We can look to five, or five million, other things and they will each leave us empty, hungry and thirsty for something else and something more.

With so many aspects of Christmas, it can be hard to keep up with what it is exactly that we are celebrating. It is perfectly great that we can enjoy the decorations, songs and time with our family and friends. It is so enjoyable to have the chance to give gifts, celebrate with Christmas parties and experience all that the season entails. It is also fun and exciting to bring your kids to see Santa, and if you are in New York City by all means see Santa at Macy's.

But what we are really celebrating comes down to one thing and one thing only.

The Lamb of God who was born to take away the sins of the world.

There is no celebration of any of the other parts of Christmas, without this as the centerpiece.

There is no joy. There is no peace. There is certainly no hope. The Lamb of God was born to take away our sins, to bring us life again.

- What competes for your focus during the Christmas season?

- What is one way you can keep the celebration centered on the arrival of Jesus?

DECEMBER 16

For unto you is born this day in the city of David a Savior, who is Christ the Lord. – **Luke 2:11**

A few years ago, we had lunch at a cafe in Brooklyn after our church service. While Jenna and the girls finished lunch, I left the restaurant and went to a previously scheduled meeting.

I thought nothing more about it until two mornings later when Jenna woke up and let me know that I needed to take money for a tip to give to the waitress that had served us two days earlier.

Jenna explained that she had placed the cost of the meal on our credit card, but the cafe did not allow for tips to be placed on the card.

Later that morning, I walked into the cafe and immediately saw the waitress who had served us on Sunday. I smiled and began explaining how we had been in the restaurant a couple days earlier, that she had waited on our family and that we did not have any cash with us to leave a tip. She remembered us and commented on how nice Jenna had been. She then said, "I think your wife said that you were the pastor of a church?" I acknowledged that I was a pastor and then I waited, curious to see where the question may have been leading.

She said, "Ever since your wife told me that you were a pastor, I was thinking there was a question I wanted to ask you." The waitress went on to tell me that she had a secret that she had been carrying for 11 years. She opened up to me about what she had done, and she let me know that she had never shared this secret with anyone. She then asked me if I thought that God was able to forgive her for such a thing.

I looked around at the cafe that was completely decorated for Christmas, and I shared with her about the depth of the love of Jesus. I shared with her the incredible grace that Jesus offers us and the freedom that is found in His forgiveness. I shared with her about the sacrifice of Jesus and why the celebration of Christmas is truly so exciting and so important.

Two weeks later on Christmas Eve we walked into the cafe and our daughter Avery walked up to the waitress, handing her a gift bag filled with cookies we had made and a colored picture of the Nativity scene. Our waitress burst into tears and from that day forward, every time that we walked into the cafe, she would come up to us and give us a big hug.

She knew that we knew her deepest, darkest secret. But that was not the end of her story. There was a greater story at work. There was a greater plan for redemption.

What makes the Christmas story so amazing is that God takes all of our stories and weaves them into His story.

No matter where we have been. No matter what we have done. There is a greater story at work. There is a greater story to be told.

Every year, we celebrate that the Christmas story changes our own story. That is worth celebrating on Christmas and every day of the year.

- What is one way that your story has been changed because of the arrival of Jesus?

- Who needs to know that their story is still being written because of the arrival of Jesus?

DECEMBER 17

May the God of hope fill you with all joy and peace in believing, so that by the power of the Holy Spirit you may abound in hope. - **Romans 15:13**

I will admit it. There have been some instances when I have watched my girls open their Christmas presents and I have been as surprised at what was under the wrapping paper as they were. Jenna does most of the shopping, all of the wrapping and generally has a much better read on what the girls want or need.

There are, however, also those presents that I am very much in on. I know exactly what is under the wrapping paper, I am fully aware of what is in the box, and I am filled with excitement and anticipation. I cannot wait for the girls to open the present! But my eyes are not focused on the wrapping paper, the box or even the gift itself.

My eyes are focused on my daughters' faces.

I do not want to miss seeing their eyes light up. I am on the edge of my seat watching for their reaction. I want to delight in their joy.

They are what I am present to.

How present is God to us?

If we are not careful, we can reduce Christmas to presents instead of His presence. Sometimes, I wonder if God is on the edge of His seat anticipating our response, our awareness, our response to His gift of Jesus.

The gift of Jesus Is amazing in so many ways, but God is always most interested in our RESPONSE to his gift of Jesus.

He is not asking us to sing "Joy to the World" without joy in our hearts. He is not asking us to proclaim "Peace on Earth" without experiencing His peace. I think He ultimately wants to see us understand His heart, and knowing Jesus is the way to do that.

God knows what He has given us. He is looking into our eyes to see if we recognize that
hope has a name, and it is Jesus.

In what ways have you seen the true meaning of Christmas reduced?

- How can you respond to Jesus as the precious gift that He is?

DECEMBER 18

> *In this is love, not that we have loved God but that he loved us and sent his Son to be the propitiation for our sins.* **- 1 John 4:10**

While serving as a Youth Pastor for many years, there were numerous times I took students to a camp where we would participate in team building exercises and various aspects of a ropes course.

Nearly every time we brought a group of students, there was some rendition of a trust fall. In a trust fall, the student doing the fall stands at the edge of a picnic table or another platform, crosses his or her arms, and falls straight backwards. The other 6-8 students are waiting with arms locked together to ensure the safe landing of the student who has taken the leap of faith.

One year, we were doing the trust fall and after nearly all of our young middle school students had taken a turn, their focus turned to me.

"Sterling, let us catch you," they pleaded. "We won't drop you. We promise!"

I looked around at the well-meaning students. I did not do all the math, but I was pretty sure I outweighed most of them combined.

They continued, "We trusted you; we want you to trust us."

Ever so reluctantly, I climbed to the edge of the picnic table.

I fell backwards.

They did not catch me.

Now, they did block my fall. They prevented me from a complete crash to the ground, but I do not think it would be accurate to say that they caught me.

Some of us know what this is like in real life. People have told us to trust them and even told us why we should trust them. We have trusted them, but, in some way, they did not catch us. Somewhere, trust was broken and that makes us hesitant to trust again.

- We are more reluctant to climb up on the picnic table the next time.
- We are more guarded when someone tells us to trust them.
- We are more cynical.
- We are more skeptical.

And so, we hold back.

Living a life of compete cynicism and skepticism is a path to absolute loneliness. If you are cynical, there is no one for you to trust. I get it, I know what it is to be hesitant to trust. But what I also know is that not trusting does not work either.

Jesus knows about broken trust. Jesus was betrayed. Jesus was denied. Jesus was forsaken by His disciples.

I am not just talking about the disciples in the Bible.

I personally know what it is to make a promise to God and break it. I personally know what it is to not follow through. I personally know that I have displayed behavior that is less than trustworthy. I personally know that I do not deserve the life, peace and hop that I have in Jesus and instead deserve punishment for my sin.

Jesus has never turned His back on me. Jesus has never changed His mind. Jesus has never dropped me.

God demonstrated his love by giving His only Son to take on the penalty of our sin and the debt of our sin. As much as some people love Christmas, there are plenty of us who can be jaded and cynical throughout the holiday season. God calls us to instead trust Him and live our lives fully committed to following Jesus.

For those of us who are reluctant to trust, this is not easy, but do not let the doubt, cynicism and skepticism that can easily creep in rob you of the celebration of Christmas.

Surrender; fall back; trust Him; Jesus will not let you down.

- What are some ways that cynicism can infiltrate the Christmas season?

- What is keeping you from "falling back" and trusting Jesus today?

DECEMBER 19

The people who walked in darkness
have seen a great light;
those who dwelt in a land of deep darkness,
on them has light shone.

– Isaiah 9:2

I love Christmas.

I love the idea of celebrating Christmas with family and friends. I love the idea of having the roaring fire in the fireplace while the kids unwrap their presents. I love the idea of sipping hot chocolate and enjoying sounds of the kids playing with the toys that they have just discovered on Christmas morning.

I love all of those things. The only problem with the Christmas season is, we have had several Christmases that were not Hallmark Movie worthy:

- The year when we traveled on Christmas Day, had more than a couple of travel mishaps, and ended up eating sandwiches from the Sheetz gas station for Christmas Dinner.

- The year when we were traveling and waited 90 minutes to be seated at Denny's for Christmas Dinner.
- The year when Avery was born on Christmas Day, though was not due until March 15.
- The year when I had Covid-19 and felt as sick as I have ever felt.

I love the memories I have from the Christmases that have gone off without a hitch.

But we learn more about what Christmas truly means when things do not go according to our plans. In some ways, it has been those Christmases that have not gone according to my plan that have reminded me how meaningful and miraculous Christmas truly is.

The real Christmas:

- The Christmas where Jesus stepped into our chaotic world.
- The Christmas where Jesus came to rescue us from the messes that we have made.
- The Christmas where Jesus came to rescue us from our destructive choices.
- The Christmas where Jesus came to rescue us from our sin-stained lives.
- The Christmas that reveals our need for a Savior.
- The Christmas where light broke into the darkness.
- The Christmas where God chose to become embodied among us.

Christmas may not always go according to our plans, but Christmas was never about our plan in the first place.

It was and is about God's plan.

- How are you dealing with chaos during this Christmas season?

- What are some ways your plans have been interrupted?

- In what ways can you ask God to help you focus on His plans over your plans?

DECEMBER 20

The true light, which gives light to everyone, was coming into the world. - **John 1:9**

One day, a while back, I walked into the wrong apartment. I thought I was on the floor where our apartment is located. I turned the corner to head to our apartment, approached the door and turned and walked in.

After I walked in, I stared straight ahead for a full two seconds and thought, "When did Jenna get a new Christmas tree and why did she rearrange the furniture?" Two forever seconds later I realized I was in the wrong apartment. I sheepishly said "I am so sorry" to the man in the room and hurried out the door.

My wife Jenna and daughter Avery laughed really hard when I told them and asked all these questions:

- "How could you just walk in? "
- "How did you not notice the wreath on the door was different?"
- "You did not see the apartment number?"

These were all fair questions. And they all had a simple answer: "I was not paying attention. My mind was somewhere else."

It does not take much to get us distracted, particularly when we are celebrating at Christmas.

- We celebrate the chance to spend time with our family.
- We celebrate with Christmas presents.
- We celebrate with holiday drinks and days off from school.
- We celebrate with Christmas lights.
- We celebrate with Christmas music.

There are so many things that we do and celebrate during the Christmas season that we can get distracted from celebrating the most important thing: that Jesus came to give hope to those who have none.

I know what it is to go through the motions distracted during the Christmas season. There have been sometimes when I have been distracted by the busyness of the season, other times was harried by stress associated with end of the year deadlines, and a few times when I was so tired, I just wanted to get Christmas over with.

I urge you to not let that happen to you and find yourself backing out of the door of someone else's house because you were too distracted to notice what you were doing.

More and more, my love for Christmas deepens each year, and I find it more and more difficult to articulate the gratitude, contentment and peace that comes with being present to the most important reality during the Christmas season and all the time: our hope in Jesus.

It is always there; we just have to pay attention.

- How can we become so distracted during the Christmas season that we miss its meaning?

- How can we pay more attention to the important aspects of Christmas to insure we do not miss the significance of the season?

DECEMBER 21

She will bear a son, and you shall call his name Jesus, for he will save his people from their sins." – **Matthew 1:21**

When I went after sin,
You came after me,
I wanted what I wanted,
You wanted me free

But still I stayed
In the middle of my mess
You wanted me to have more
While I was fine with less

I played and played
In the mud and mire
I had sunk so low
But you wanted to take me higher

I was stuck in my own ways
and really did not care

I ignored everything I heard you say
but you were still there.

Things started to wear thin
As I started to wear out
The lights were growing dim
And I was filled with doubt

The night never seemed to end
From darkness until dawn
Still, I heard you call to me again
That I was not too far gone

Even though I went after sin,
You still came after me
You lifted me up out of the pit
So I could be free

You showed me your love
You showed me your kindness
You ignored my shoves
You disregarded my blindness

Even when I went my own way
You still gave chase
There has never been one day
You were not pursuing me with grace

DECEMBER 22

But God, being rich in mercy, because of the great love with which he loved us, even when we were dead in our trespasses, made us alive together with Christ–by grace you have been saved–and raised us up with him and seated us with him in the heavenly places in Christ Jesus, so that in the coming ages he might show the immeasurable riches of his grace in kindness toward us in Christ Jesus. **- Ephesians 2:4-7**

There are times when I want to minimize my own sin and guilt. I want to downplay the significance of my need for a Savior and His sacrifice.

I know how to deceive myself into thinking that I am not so bad. I am able to convince myself there are others worse than me. I have entertained thoughts like "At least I am not as bad as ______."

This way of thinking is not actually true, they are only my attempt to justify myself. Still, there are moments when I forget just how desperate I am for the sacrifice that only Jesus could provide.

A while back, I was reminded about my need in an unlikely way. Jenna and I were watching a Christmas movie when a commercial came on advertising "Miracle Spring Water."

The commercial talked about how water was a big theme with Jesus concerning healing. The commercial highlighted how the Miracle Water had allowed people to buy homes, retire debt and experience unprecedented prosperity. The promises of the product combined with the association of biblical principles would have been laughable had been part of a joke. But I was really watching the Miracle Water being offered as the source of provision for people's need.

The "Miracle Water" was clearly a scam. The "Miracle Water" was utterly ridiculous.

And then, I was struck that no "Miracle Water" – no source I could come up with – was capable of addressing my deepest need: someone to save me and restore me from my sin. My need for a Savior and for His sacrifice could only be met in one way and by one person.

Jesus came to rescue us, to restore us, to redeem us and to reconcile us.

The celebration of Christmas is not commemorative. It is not just that we are looking back at a great moment in history. The celebration of Christmas is not that we pause to remember a good man who accomplished some good things.

The celebration of Christmas marks a Savior who was born to live a perfect life, die an undeserved and sacrificial death, be resurrected, and bring grace and the power of resurrection to all who place their faith, trust and hope in Him.

More than any Miracle Water, more than our best effort on our best day, more than anything that anyone can offer, Jesus supplies what no one and nothing else can.

Jesus' coming is more than enough for me, for you and for everyone who in their own brokenness and need, reaches out to the One who can save them.

- In what ways are you prone to comparing yourself to others and minimizing your sin?

- How can Christmas be celebrated with the joy and hope that Jesus came to provide?

DECEMBER 23

In him we have obtained an inheritance, having been predestined according to the purpose of him who works all things according to the counsel of his will, so that we who were the first to hope in Christ might be to the praise of his glory. – **Ephesians 1:11–12**

Christmas is more significant to me now than when I was a kid. But I have not always felt this way.

There are times in my life that I can remember with fondness the magic and mystery that would accompany Christmas morning. I remember the anticipation of what gifts may be underneath the wrapping paper.

I remember the wonder that would follow in somehow getting a present that I had wanted but had never said anything about out loud. I remember the amazement that would come with a special present that exceeded all expectations. Those were great times that I cherish from my childhood.

But Christmas means more to me now.

Christmas means more to me now because I have a much greater understanding of why Jesus came and why

He had to come. It is possible to celebrate the birth of Jesus in a historical way, remembering the birth of Jesus. We can read and recite the details of Mary, the manger and the Magi. I have spent many Christmases focusing on these historical realities, and these are undoubtedly important concerning the birth of Jesus. I have learned and celebrated so many of these aspects of Christmas since I was a kid.

But as an adult, I am captivated by other elements of the birth of Jesus. The significance of God's love. The promise of hope. The preciousness of peace.

I am captivated by the fact that the motive for Jesus being born was love for me. And I know that it is not just love for me that led Jesus to come. He came to make salvation available to the entire world. I am still amazed that God loved me and others enough to send His Son as a baby into our world.

It is amazing that God orchestrated a plan from the beginning of time to bring forth the historical event of a Savior being born to a woman who was a virgin. But, just as amazing, is the personal reality that God really loves me.

Why is that so amazing to me? Because I am not so lovable. I am certainly not deserving of love. I fall short. I do not actually do all of the things that I say I will do. At times, I end up doing the very thing that I say that I will not do.

And, still, Jesus loves me.

Christmas amazes me now because hope is not found in a thing. Hope was born in a lowly manger, on a quiet night, in Bethlehem. As an adult I appreciate my hope in Jesus more than ever. The love of God and the hope that I have in Jesus has brought me real and lasting peace.

The mystery and wonder at Christmas still exist for me. The amazement of God's grace is still profound. The anticipation of His mercies made new every morning is better than any gift under the tree. My prayer is that every year of my life will bring me to a greater and greater appreciation of just how incredible Christmas is as I continue to discover just how much I need a Savior and how Jesus is the all-sufficient provision for that need.

- How have you grown to appreciate the Christmas season?

- In what ways has your love or appreciation for the Christmas season changed?

DECEMBER 24

And the angel answered him, "I am Gabriel. I stand in the presence of God, and I was sent to speak to you and to bring you this good news. – **Luke 1:19**

On Christmas Eve, my kids desperately want to know what is under the Christmas Tree. They are ready to open their presents and they are pleading for any type of hint as to what is in them.

And the truth is, I want to tell them all about it! I want to blurt out what the presents are and celebrate with them. I can honestly say that I am probably more excited about them opening up the Christmas presents than they are to open them. But, for one more day, I refrain from revealing to them what is wrapped under the shiny paper.

Think about what it must have been like for Zechariah when he was told that he and his wife Elizabeth would become parents. Zechariah questioned the angel Gabriel by asking him how this could occur since he and Elizabeth were so old.

I love the response of Gabriel to Zechariah. Quite simply, Gabriel says, "This is how I know. I am Gabriel and I stand in the presence of God" (Luke 1:19).

Gabriel had incredible, life-changing news to share with Zechariah. But, in light of Zechariah not believing, Gabriel let him know that he would not be able to speak until the birth of his son John.

I cannot imagine anything being harder for Zechariah than not being able to share the good news. I know how excited I get just to share about one gift that the girls are getting. For Zechariah, it must have been incredibly difficult. The thing that he had prayed for hundreds, if not thousands of times, was happening.

He was about to be a father. Elizabeth was about to be a mother.

I am certain that Zechariah wanted to tell every friend, neighbor and stranger on the street that God had responded that God had answered his prayer, and that a baby boy was on the way. Yet, for months, he could only use hand motions or draw in the dirt or on a tablet to convey the news.

In contrast to the secret of Christmas presents, the message of Christmas is meant to be told and proclaimed openly. We do not have to wait until Christmas Day to reveal the incredible gift that God has given us in His Son Jesus. We do not have to wait to talk about God's response to our desperate need. We have been given a gift, and with that gift, we have been given a message of hope.

And that message of hope is for everyone, everywhere.

Let's not wait to share the incredible news that Jesus Christ is born to take away the sins of the world. We have every reason to celebrate and proclaim every day of the year that we are liberated because of this glorious truth.

- How is the hope of Jesus impacting you this Christmas season?

- What is the Good News that you can share with others this Christmas season and in any season?

DECEMBER 25

Though you have not seen him, you love him. Though you do not now see him, you believe in him and rejoice with joy that is inexpressible and filled with glory, obtaining the outcome of your faith, the salvation of your souls.

– 1 Peter 1:8-9

As a child, I grew up in Houston, Texas, and I loved Christmas. Christmas was always a big deal in our family. I remember many Christmas days when we could go over to my grandparents on my dad's side of the family for breakfast and later go over to my grandparents on my mom's side of the family for lunch.

These were always great times to see our family and we loved opening Christmas presents with both sides of the family. Throughout the day, the main thought was that the "real" Christmas presents were going to be opened by me and my brother after we got back home sometime that evening.

In the evolution of becoming an adult and a parent, the focus of the Christmas presents has changed. I have come to appreciate the pleasure of watching my own children open presents more than the joy that comes with being the opener. I love the excitement of seeing my kids' faces. The anticipation of knowing what they do not know and watching their eyes open wide as they realize what is beneath the wrapping paper in the box.

We love to give our kids presents and it is so much fun to share these moments with our family.

But my evolution concerning the joy of Christmas has expanded to include much more.

Christmas includes time with family, lights and presents. Christmas includes finding bargains, holiday drinks and days off from school. All the trappings of the season can be somewhat confusing.

It is confusing because I like all of these elements and there is nothing wrong with any of them. But over the last few years the celebration of Christmas has become something more to me.

- I understand more my desperate need for God's grace.
- I understand more my desperate need for a Savior.
- I understand more that my independent way of doing life does not work and I understand that my pursuits do not satisfy.
- I understand that my deepest and most personal need was met when God sent His Son Jesus on a rescue mission to save me.

That is the enduring hope of Christmas and the lasting joy of Christmas. And it is available to you as well.

The joy of Christmas is not the hype. It is not the trappings of the season. It is the realization of the truth that God sees me, and God sees you.

God sees.

God responds.

This is what we are celebrating at Christmas and this celebration leaves me with a joy that goes beyond words. In so many ways, it is a joy that I cannot describe.

But I can sum it up this way:

Hope has a Name! His name is Jesus!

Merry Christmas!

- How can you celebrate the coming off Jesus this Christmas season?

- What part of His coming stands out to you as we enter into a new year?

ABOUT THE AUTHOR

Sterling Edwards and his wife, Jenna, have four amazing daughters, one spectacular son in-law, and two incredible grandsons. Sterling is a pastor and a church planting catalyst with the North American Mission Board. After spending thirteen years church planting in New York, Sterling and his family currently serve in Phoenix, Arizona.

WHAT IS THE CHURCH?
AND, WHY IS IT SO IMPORTANT?

MARK HALLOCK
& AARON WEBER

Made in the USA
Las Vegas, NV
03 March 2025

18970608R00056